Pebble®

Dogs

Yorkshire Terriers

by Joanne Linden

Consulting Editor: Gail Saunders-Smith, PhD

Consultant: Jennifer Zablotny, DVM
Member, American Veterinary Medical Association

Capstone
press®
Mankato, Minnesota

Pebble Books are published by Capstone Press,
151 Good Counsel Drive, P.O. Box 669, Mankato, Minnesota 56002.
www.capstonepress.com

1 2 3 4 5 6 11 10 09 08 07 06

Library of Congress Cataloging-in-Publication Data
Linden, Joanne.
    Yorkshire terriers / by Joanne Linden.
    p. cm.— (Pebble. Dogs)
    Includes bibliographical references and index.
    ISBN-13: 978-0-7368-6329-2 (hardcover)
    ISBN-10: 0-7368-6329-X (hardcover)
    1. Yorkshire terrier—Juvenile literature. I. Title. II. Series: Pebble Books. Dogs.
SF429.Y6L55 2007
636.76—dc22   2005037365

Summary: Simple text and photographs introduce the Yorkshire terrier breed, its
growth from puppy to adult, and pet care information.

Note to Parents and Teachers

The Dogs set supports national science standards related to life
science. This book describes and illustrates Yorkshire terriers.
The images support early readers in understanding the text. The
repetition of words and phrases helps early readers learn new
words. This book also introduces early readers to subject-specific
vocabulary words, which are defined in the Glossary section. Early
readers may need assistance to read some words and to use the
Table of Contents, Glossary, Read More, Internet Sites, and Index
sections of the book.

Table of Contents

Yorkies 5
From Puppy to Adult 11
Taking Care of Yorkies 17

Glossary 22
Read More 23
Internet Sites 23
Index 24

4

Yorkies

The first Yorkshire Terriers came from Yorkshire, England. These dogs are called Yorkies.

Long ago, Yorkies
hunted rats.
Today, they are friendly
lapdogs who like
to be with people.

Some Yorkies compete
in dog shows. They race
through tricky courses.
Judges also give prizes
to the most beautiful dogs.

From Puppy to Adult

Newborn Yorkies are only as big as a mouse. Their eyes don't open until they are a few weeks old.

Black and tan fur
covers Yorkie puppies.
Their hair is short
and frizzy when
they are young.

Adult Yorkies grow long, silky hair. Their color changes to steel blue and tan.

Taking Care of Yorkies

Owners should brush their Yorkies every day.
A topknot or bow keeps long hair out
of a Yorkie's face.

Yorkies eat only a little bit of dog food each day. They need lots of water after playing.

Yorkies chase and play
with their owners.
They never seem
to get tired.

Glossary

course—a set path; dogs compete on courses with tunnels, jumps, and turns.

dog show—a contest or performance where dogs compete in shows for beauty and running courses

England—a country in Europe that is part of the United Kingdom

lapdog—a very small dog that wants to be near its owner and sit on laps

steel blue—a very dark blue or blackish color

topknot—the hair on a dog's head that is tied back with a small rubber band and often a bow

Read More

Stone, Lynn M. *Yorkshire Terriers.* Eye to Eye with Dogs. Vero Beach, Fla.: Rourke, 2005.

Trumbauer, Lisa. *The Life Cycle of a Dog.* Life Cycles. Mankato, Minn.: Capstone Press, 2002.

Internet Sites

FactHound offers a safe, fun way to find Internet sites related to this book. All of the sites on FactHound have been researched by our staff.

Here's how:

1. Visit *www.facthound.com*
2. Choose your grade level.
3. Type in this book ID **073686329X** for age-appropriate sites. You may also browse subjects by clicking on letters, or by clicking on pictures and words.
4. Click on the **Fetch It** button.

FactHound will fetch the best sites for you!   23

Index

brushing, 17
color, 13, 15
dog shows, 9
eyes, 11
food, 19
hair, 13, 15, 17

hunting, 7
lapdogs, 7
owners, 17, 21
puppies, 11, 13
water, 19
Yorkshire, England, 5

Word Count: 150
Grade: 1
Early-Intervention Level: 14

Editorial Credits
Heather Adamson, editor; Juliette Peters, set designer; Ted Williams, book designer; Kelly Garvin, photo researcher/photo editor

Photo Credits
Animal photography, 14
Capstone Press/Karon Dubke, 6, 16, 18, 20
Cheryl A. Ertelt, 4
Norvia Behling, 1
Ron Kimball Stock/Ron Kimball, cover
Shutterstock/Steven Pepple, 12
Superstock/Geri Lavrow, 10
Visuals Unlimited/Cheryl Ertelt, 8